Wit and Wisdom

Find Your Author Strength

Craig Martelle

Craig Martelle, Inc

Exclusively in ebook form as an early release for Kevin J. Anderson's Author Tools Storybundle, September-October 2024

An exclusive first release in print for Superstars Writing Seminars 2025

Printed by BookVault

Available worldwide on Amazon starting in February 28, 2025.

Published by Craig Martelle, Inc

PO Box 10235

Fairbanks, AK 99710

Contents

Foreword

By Kevin J. Anderson

There used to be a playbook for writers—a standard career path, a sequence of steps you knew you had to take in order to work your way up and maybe, eventually, rarely, become a success.

It was just like having a career as a doctor, lawyer, or banker. It was a lot of work, but there was a mutually agreed-upon roadmap to follow.

I knew I wanted to be a writer from the time I was a kid. So, I studied those expectations and got in line, ready to do what I had to do. It was akin to becoming an Olympic athlete: You began with a certain amount of talent. You practiced. You worked. You competed. If you got good enough, and lucky enough, you might proceed to the next stage.

Every aspiring science fiction writer started out writing short stories and submitting them to magazines, usually getting a few published in a small press, and finally breaking into a professional magazine. With enough of those credits under your belt, you could find an agent and then send him your novel manuscript, and maybe he'd sell it to one of the big houses.

I did all those things. I had dozens of stories published in fanzines or small press publications. Finally, in 1985, I secured my first pro sale in The Magazine of Fantasy and Science Fiction, then got an agent who sold my first novel, which was published by Signet Books in 1988. I was offered a multi-book contract, and then another one. Eventually, I started writing novels for Star Wars and Lucasfilm, had my first New York Times bestseller in 1993. And I was off to the races.

With each step of the process, I left 90% of my colleagues behind. Only so many could make it. Becoming a traditionally successful science fiction author was like surviving multiple rounds of the Squid Game. In order to be picked for that one lead slot of the publisher's releases, everyone else had to lose.

I had it made, though. Now that I had climbed to the summit of Mount Olympus, trad publishers were throwing more book contracts at me than I could possibly accept. I had seven New York Times bestsellers in one year. I was translated into 32 languages, eventually ending up with 24 million copies in print and 58 national or international bestsellers. I was even disparaged as a "hack" because I wrote more than a couple books a year.

I had it made.

Never, ever believe you have it made.

I didn't count on the entire publishing world being turned upside down. Around 2010, all the rules began to change. The Borders bookstore chain collapsed, taking with it half of the bookshelves in the country, with some of the biggest casualties being genre fiction. The mass-market paperback book segment collapsed, and that was where I'd done most of my work. My media tie-in projects—all my Star Wars, X-Files, movie novelizations, Star Trek, Batman, and Starcraft work—disappeared practically overnight. The market just wasn't there.

But I was aware enough of the field and paid attention to the business aspects that I saw these huge changes coming. I looked up in the sky and spotted the giant asteroid hurtling toward us—so I decided to evolve and become a mammal instead of a dinosaur.

Those were the early days of indie publishing, and it was all terra incognita, with new technology, new markets, and new rules. I founded my own publishing house, reissued all my out-of-print backlist, as well as many books from my friends, who were also big-name authors. I had to figure this out, but now there wasn't any playbook. It was like running through a deadly obstacle course in total darkness.

Then I discovered an even more earth-shaking paradigm shift. Nobody knew the rules! We were all trying different things, experimenting—and discovering that the unshakable, eternal verities of traditional publishing and bookselling might have been set in stone, but they weren't exactly true and proven. A lot of these people were coming into the publishing world fresh, with no baggage and no preconceptions, and they were trying to understand how it all worked.

Even more importantly, I saw that succeeding in indie publishing wasn't like the Squid Game. These ambitious authors were discovering new things, and they loved to share them openly. They wanted to help explore this new world.

Craig Martelle was at the vanguard running Michael Anderle's open and vibrant group of 20Booksto50k®, with his workshops and lectures and constant mentoring. He was paying it forward—and he didn't even have a traditional publishing track record to pay it back.

The information Craig exchanged was unheard of from my trad background. He and other successful indie authors revealed their actual numbers—wow, real data!—and earnest advice without a second thought, without wondering what was in it for them. Craig shared and encouraged, he coached, he critiqued, and he walked the walk.

I first met Craig in person in 2018, a few years after he became a full-time indie author, but I already knew who he was. I had read his postings and learned from them, adapted his advice to my own circumstances. We've become very good friends in the meantime. He's invited me to speak multiple times at the 20Books Conference in Las Vegas, as well as in Bali and Aruba. Craig has taught several times at my own Superstars Writing Seminar in Colorado Springs.

Every time I go to one of these conferences, I feel like my head is going to explode. I come home with notebooks filled with notes and bullet points of things I should be trying, new ideas that should have been obvious, and other ones that seem utterly impossible, and yet they work.

We don't get paid for this. We just do it, because that's what you're supposed to do. Craig comes from a career in the Marines and has a law degree, and although those experiences inform his decisions and his advice, the depth of it comes from his heart.

I can barely keep up with the successes this army of indie authors who are killing it. When Craig invited me to be a guest speaker again, I asked him what I could possibly teach these dynamos. He insisted that information sharing was a two-way street, though I have to confess, I feel more like a frontage road, while the other direction is an interstate highway.

But I wholeheartedly endorse Craig's core philosophy that a rising tide lifts all boats. It's not a Squid Game. It's a team effort, and we all benefit, writers and readers.

This book is filled with numerous short and digestible gems of Craig's philosophy, his suggestions, and alternatives you may not have considered. These vital ideas may seem simple and obvious, and yet you need to internalize them.

"Don't half-ass what could be the best career you'll ever have."

"There's no such thing as perfect."

Or deceptively powerful commandments like "Be kind in all things."

Read all of these nuggets, and if you "get" only a tenth of them and implement them, then you'll be a richer writer, publisher, and human being for it.

Chapter 1 – Stuff

GET UP. SHOW UP. Do the Work.

Talent is important, but using it is what separates the wildly successful from the pack. You can get far in this business by showing up and working hard at the right things. Becoming a better storyteller takes practice. There's no practice like writing stories that your fans will like until they love them. As for the business side of it, Nike has the right tagline. Just do it. You don't have to love the business and marketing, you just have to do them.

Your Words Have Value

Even your early words when you didn't write your best material. Being an author is a business where you get paid to practice. Write better and better, but you'll still be able to sell your early work. Readers are forgiving, especially if you tell a good story.

Don't Half-ass What Could Be the Best Career You'll Ever Have

Being a professional author takes work. You can't just wing it, even though you may feel that way while writing. Enjoy the process of story-telling, but do the other stuff, too. You'll find that others take a huge cut of work that you can easily do for yourself. Don't limit your viability as a professional by putting yourself into a small box.

Fear Should Motivate Us, Not Paralyze Us

Too many are afraid of publishing that first book. What are you afraid of? A bruised ego? You're venturing into the world of being a public person. You're going to get both good and bad feedback. Take the good and get better. Learn from the bad, even if it seems hurtful. It tells you that you may not have hit your exact target audience. Adjust and put it in better readers' hands while simultaneously writing better books.

A Rising Tide Lifts All Boats

A quote from John F. Kennedy that supports the challenge and success of being an author. No one has to lose for me to win. No one has to lose for anyone to win. Winning is personal, just like writing a book, but just because you write alone doesn't mean you are alone. Authors are better together, supporting each other. It's amazing what happens with a few kind words. Another way to say it is that we all win together.

Self-publishing Is a Learning Journey

It's best undertaken with intentionality to get better at those things that need to be done better. You don't have to love all parts of the business, but you do need to understand them. And the parts you do love, keep loving them, otherwise it becomes painful and something you want to escape from rather than escape to.

Your Eyes Look Forward. That's a Hint for Life.

Businesses that spend too much time looking back will get stuck in the past. Once you learn the lesson that history has taught you, keep your eyes straight ahead. So what that you managed nine one-star reviews in a row because you uploaded the wrong version of your manuscript? You know what not to do and you've fixed it. You can lament the error, or you can let your readers know and have a good laugh. Then move on. The windshield is so much larger than the rearview mirror. There's a good reason for that. The real obstacles are in front of you.

Marketing Has Three Pillars

Advertising, promotions, and brand. Ads will put your work in front of potential readers through passive product placement where they might be browsing. Promotions are active efforts to put those books in front of potential readers, such as paid newsletters. Brand is how a potential reader feels when they see your name/books. If it's positive, you can make a sale without an ad or promotion.

Little Wins Keep You Going

Don't look for the big wins. Set inchstones instead of milestones and revel in reaching them and bounding forward, one inchstone at a time.

Maintain Balance

You can't write if your brain is mush. You have to balance your health and well-being with the business of being an author. Maintain the level of fitness that's right for you and control your diet. Cheetos and Diet Coke won't help your body operate at max efficiency. Your bones and muscles exist as the meat wagon to drive your brain around. Make the best of it.

You Write Your Own Story

You are the master of your story. Don't let someone else take it over and dictate to you what you're about. That is in your hands. You determine who you are. People will judge you on what they see. Do your actions mirror your intent? If you want to write a book, then write a book. Saying you want to write but never writing is anathema to being a writer. Writers write.

Write with the Reader in Mind

This is also called write to market. It's not a huge shift from writing what you want, but you have to keep the reader in mind while you're crafting your characters and telling your tale. Your readers will be the final arbiters if you've succeeded. They vote with their money, and you want their votes. You're not selling out if you don't write just what you want. It's still your story. Successful authors understand their readers and give them what they want.

Write a Great Book. Put it in the Right Readers' Hands.

These are the two things you need to do if you want a successful author career. Simple, right? There might be a few moving parts under each, but when you boil it down to the basics, this is it. If you write a good book in a great way, that will also be compelling for your readership. Always build your reader foundation. Nothing is more important than your readers, and nothing will increase your revenue more quickly than selling your entire catalogue to one reader, over and over again.

Writing Is a Lonely Profession, but You Don't Have to Be Alone

Find writers' groups. There are millions of authors out there, some are better than others in keeping you motivated to do your own thing. As long as you're not looking for someone to carry you, you'll find those people who will help you. But that help will look like motivation and support, not individuals who are selling your books for you. Those people generally don't exist. If it's too good to be true, don't believe it. You are the master of your destiny. Don't hand that to anyone else.

If You Don't Pay for the Product, You Are the Product.

I heard this from Mal Cooper, and it resonated. Lots of 'free' products out there. Free to use, but know that you have given up something to get them. Is it your email? Is it your usage history (for their marketing)? Is it your products? Google Docs is a great way to share, but understand that you've handed over all your material to a company. You own the copyright to your work, but you've licensed Google to do things with it. I'd rather pay for the product and not wonder how the 'free' provider is using it or me.

The Motivation of Sales

Hell yeah! There's nothing like selling your book to strangers to boost your spirits. When that paycheck hits the bank, life feels pretty good. Sales help keep us motivated, but even the biggest authors started with making that first sale. For many, it was getting through the gates to a traditional publishing house. For others, it was through self-publishing. And for all, it was the sale of your story, your work, and the entertainment it provided to those strangers.

Don't Include Words That Make the Reader Want to Stop Reading

A little wisdom from Elmore Leonard. Enter the scene late and leave early. That keeps the readers engaged. If you overstay your welcome, then you're going to lose readers. They tend not to come back, too. Keep them reading from start to finish. Lose the uninteresting parts of your book, no matter how much you love those errant words.

Quantity Has a Quality All its Own

Quality matters a great deal in this business because that keeps the readers coming back for more. With quantity, you can revise, refine, and improve. Sell that burgeoning backlist while you move forward with better and better titles. I'll harp on this throughout this book, because the way you get better at writing is to write, and many readers read fast and want more.

I Read My Reviews

People are psychopaths. And they're reading your stuff. Some will become fanatical followers and others will be casual observers, lurkers, who pick up a title of yours every now and then. They all have something to say because the anonymity of the internet allows them that privilege. Read between the lines and find the nuggets that will help you become a better storyteller. Many reviews will be kind but can't be mined for gold. Others will be mean spirited, but that says more about the reviewer than you. Pity those poor souls and move on.

You Work for Yourself, but You Don't

You work for whoever pays your wages. From the time you started working and getting paid, you worked for someone else. Even CEOs (which is what you are in your author business) work for someone else—the shareholders. In our business, that means our readers. Give them what they'll buy and make them like it because it's good. If you write whatever you like and think they'll buy it no matter what, you'll find out that you may be wrong. You can write what you like but temper it by keeping those readers in mind. Unless you don't care about being paid, then do whatever you want, regardless of the consequences.

Price Your Books to Make a Profit

This is a complex question with lots of ifs and buts, but in the end, you have to make money if you're going to stay in business. If you have one book and you offer it for free, you make no money. If you have three books in one series, you can offer the first for free, trusting that readers will like it enough to pick up the next two. Or you can price all your books in a way to make a profit. The higher the price point, the fewer books you'll sell until you have a huge readership and a solid brand for delivering quality stories. Lots of things to think about with pricing, but don't get your readers used to you giving your books away or offering steep discounts.

Gotta Get the Words

If you don't write your books, you have nothing to sell. A store with a single product on the shelves won't do as well as a store that's fully stocked with a variety of good stuff.

The Story Is Inspired

When you get a story idea that appears in a vision, can you see a whole story out of it or just the punchline? Maybe just the setup? Inspiration can be nurtured with an idea until you have a start, a middle, and a conclusion with great high points. Then you have to get down to the pedestrian work of writing the whole thing. Not every word of a story will be inspired. I suspect very little is, but that inspiration is profound. Wrap a great story around it using well-practiced and smooth prose.

Write Down Your Great Ideas

Inspiration strikes at odd times. If you think you'll remember those great ideas, you're probably going to let yourself down. Write a sentence or two, or leave a voice memo on your watch or your phone. It takes seconds to immortalize your grandest thoughts. You'll know where you wanted to go with the idea. Some have legs, and some don't. It's better to have them all together so you can choose wisely in how to best invest your writing time.

Author Peers

As a professional author, your peers are every other author. At author conferences, you'll see them standing next to you. A few accolades go a long way. "I loved your (say title to show that you're not making it up)." That's all it takes. A seasoned pro will ask what you write. Share briefly without self-denigration. "I write sci-fi and thrillers. I've sold over a million books but can't tell you which gets the better long-term traction. Only been in the business eight years. Thank you for leading the way." Or something like that. Simple and quick.

Don't Get Lost in the Noise

There is more data than you can use. Too much is overwhelming. You don't need most of it and analyzing it to micro detail is unnecessary in nearly all cases. Don't sweat the micro-load. Go for the macro view of the world. Give your brain a rest. Are you making more money than you're spending? That's the first measure of success. You can refine once you see what gives you the greatest payback for your time. Remember Pareto—eighty percent of your revenue will come from twenty percent of your efforts. Find what works. Do more of that.

Chapter 2– More Stuff

HOOK YOUR READER WITH the First Sentence

In this day and age, attention spans range from that of a goldfish (ten seconds) to even less. It's easy for a reader to move on as they all have to-be-read piles that stretch into the stratosphere. Why do they keep reading? You hook them with intrigue and adventure. You tell them what the story's about in a single sentence that forms a question in the reader's mind. You set the tone and introduce the world. The reader has to keep reading to find out more.

If You're Not Crying When You Write It, then Your Readers Won't When They Read It

Readers may not necessarily remember your words, but they will remember how you made them feel. Grip them well.

The Worlds Inside Our Minds Are the Only and Best Refuge

It's okay to dwell there. What do your superfans say? Your words take them away. From your mind to theirs. No matter what else is going on in either of your lives. Although your meat wagon may be getting rusty, don't let the mind it hauls lose its edge. Bring worlds to life through your words. Keep your mind sharp. Restore the edge with new adventures, even if you don't leave your home.

Write the First Chapter and the Last Chapter, then Write All the Stuff in Between

The first chapter is where the readers decide if they want to keep reading. (See above.) The last chapter is your light at the end of the tunnel. It tells you where you're going. If you know where you're going, you can get there. Easy as that. Fill in the rest of the chapters along the backbone of your story, adding side plots and subplots as needed to give you the length you want for your book. Know where you're going with the story. It's the most important thing you can do. The rest falls into place.

The First Chapter Sells This Book. The Last Chapter Sells the Next Book. (Mickey Spillane)

I believe this one with all my heart. If you leave the reader with a great feeling at the end of the book, they'll be looking for the next one. A story that a reader can't put down followed by an immediate purchase of the next book in the series. That is the highest testament to quality. It is perfection for that one reader at that single moment in time. Find more like that person. Lots more. Build a relationship with these good people and the heavy lifting of marketing will not be so heavy. Always end strong.

Be Kind in All Things

It takes a little practice, but being kind generally costs you nothing. It doesn't mean be a pushover.

It's about not snapping at people or criticizing. You don't need to fix other people. You can only control one person, and that's you. How you respond to situations is who you really are. Be kind. It'll save you from having to apologize later.

Your Current Valley Is Someone Else's Peak

Are your book sales getting you down? What have you done to keep them juiced? The bad news about this business is that you'll be forgotten if you don't keep your books in front of readers, both new and existing. New covers. New promotions. New titles. New reader engagement. Stay relevant and your lows will climb.

Why Are You an Author?

Never forget why you became an author. It'll carry your through the middle of a story that is dragging. It'll carry you through a book that doesn't seem to sell well. It'll keep you going when everyone is telling you to stop. Your internal motivation is what will take you from failure to success.

Write Better with Each New Word

Are you reading? Are you getting feedback about your words? Are you learning to write better and better? Writing is not an inherent talent. I will argue that storytelling is innate, but writing it down absolutely is not. That means you have to practice. Write with intent. Get trusted readers in your genre to keep you on the straight and narrow. Sometimes, technically correct writing is boring. Verbs and subjects must agree, but you might not always need a verb or a noun. You need the story to flow. You need characters that readers can relate to.

There's Never Been a Better Time to be an Author

You hear the doom and gloom and stories about the glory days of publishing and blah, blah, blah. Don't listen to that garbage. Every day is a different day. The knowledge available to every single potential author is nearly overwhelming. When I started in 2015, people were already talking about the "good ole days." I've sold over a million books in my short career without having one go viral. That should tell you everything you need to know.

Hope Is a Lousy Plan

I learned that one in the Marine Corps. The only kind of plan is a plans plan. Map out the steps you need to take to get where you want to go. Check the boxes along that route and surprise! Look how lucky you've been. Luck is the product of hard work aligning with opportunity. 'I hope I'll get something done' isn't the same as 'I'll get these four things done first and then that one.'

You Can Always Sell a Good Book

You may not sell it right away because you didn't put it in front of the right readers, but that doesn't mean you can't sell it. Maybe a publisher will pick it up. Maybe a new cover and blurb will juice it. The story has to carry the day. The story is what brings readers on board your brand. When you get a reader to love one of your books, they will give you the benefit of the doubt on the rest. Find them and let your good book carry sales through to your other good books.

Routine Is Your Friend

With a routine, you can block out your writing time, admin time, marketing time, all of it. You can make sure you've given yourself the head space to do what your business needs. Your family will learn about your boundaries if you strictly reinforce them, giving yourself the fifteen minutes a day (or more) that you can devote to your author business. Just fifteen a day is the start of a great routine.

Write Every Day

Some people can get away with not writing every day, but I write because I need to. If you write every day, then the words add up fast. A thousand words a day is four long novels a year. When I'm rolling, I can get a thousand words in thirty minutes. And I love writing. Writing every day works for me. Writing is fifty percent or more of my overall business. I spend more than half my time writing.

There's No Such Thing as Perfect

It's in the eyes of the beholder—as in, the reader—and as we've all seen, not all stories appeal to all readers. Even the best books out there have one-star reviews. Sure, you can chalk it up to trolls, but you can reword your sentence a hundred times and it'll still never be perfect. It could always be different. Don't hamstring yourself thinking your work isn't perfect. It isn't and never will be. It only needs to be the best you can make it on any given day. Or you can sabotage yourself by diddling with it until it's raw and bleeding and unpresentable to the public.

Forgive Yourself

You've done something that occupies too much of your mind. If you're going to move forward, you have to stop looking back. Free your thoughts to focus on building a strong foundation for the future of your business. A free mind is far more creative. Remove the shackles and see how far you are capable of going.

'Maybe' Is the Worst Word an Author Can Say

When you commit your business to *maybe*, you're not only giving yourself permission to fail, you're actively promoting failure. "Maybe" isn't a plan, and it's not a step that will help you reach a goal. If you fail while striding across the stepping stones to success, you can add steps, take a different step, or start over, but failure in this sense isn't failure at all. It's learning what does and doesn't work. A definite "maybe" is a tentative possibility that you'll get nothing from your work—not learning, not even marginal success. You're counting on luck to get you where you want to go, and lady luck probably won't be there when you need her most.

Decide to Be Happy

Happiness is a decision. Decide early in the day that you're going to be happy and don't let anything dissuade you. It's too easy to be angry all the time. Sometimes, spite can be a good motivator, but it will only work for a short time, then you need something a little more substantive. It's okay to worry, but it's also okay to be happy about what you have and how far you've come in life. If you're reading this, you have a perfect record of making it through the day to see tomorrow.

Life Balance

You have to have it. You can't be one hundred percent in on writing. For most humans, you can't write all day every day. Your brain needs to rest, and your body is the meat wagon that drives your brain around, so you need that to be fully functional, too. Maybe cut down on processed foods and sugars. Treat your body well and it'll treat your mind well. A sound mind makes the process of creating stories better. Be the best storyteller you can be. Revel in letting the bone-framed meat wagon support that fabulous mind of yours.

Small Steps

What small step can you take today to help yourself? It's important to never stop moving. Don't feel bad about putting yourself first, even if it's only for a few minutes. When you have that time, what do you? If it's more, what do you do? Small steps add up over time to become a great journey. Make the most from your life's adventure.

Fear of AI

So-called AI is not going to replace you. Don't fear the unknown boogeyman. Your words will be your voice. Write and write some more. Your creativity cannot be replicated by a machine. Don't let fear paralyze your efforts to become an author. "What's the use? We're going to get buried under AI-written books. I'm wasting my time." The way to success is by building a readership for your good books. The way to failure is giving up before you've given yourself a chance to be a professional author.

New Author Traction

How do you get those initial readers when you publish your first book? By being a part of the community. If you've participated in support groups for authors, in reading groups (not promoting your book) by being kind with your words and gracious in spirit, then when you ask people to give your book a read, they will repay kindness with kindness. Don't be mercenary about it by demanding a quid pro quo. It only takes one stranger's voice to make the difference in your mindset.

Why Am I Doing This?

I retired from the Marine Corps after twenty years. That was completely different from being an author, but it provided all the fodder I needed for a lifetime of stories with good humor. I retired a second time at age 52 and started writing full-time. This is an incredibly fulfilling career and a better legacy. I needed a lifetime's worth of experience to realize my destiny. Maybe your time to be an author isn't right now, but if you keep writing, practicing your craft, and learning the author business, you'll launch into the stratosphere when it *is* your time.

Recognizing Burnout

Burnout is an ugly beast. You can recognize when it's coming and avoid it, or it will declare itself at the most inopportune time. Signs of burnout include taking more time to do less, loss of joy, pain when looking at your manuscript (physical and emotional), feeling out of control, and I'm sure you know more of your own "tells." Revise your deadlines and step back. Give yourself grace while understanding the difference between pushing too hard and disappointment in sales. One requires a vacation while the other needs a more in-depth business analysis as to why you're not selling.

Are You Holding Yourself to the Right Standard?

Everyone starts writing thinking that they can emulate their favorite author. Most likely, you can't. Don't rate your first foray into authordom at the same level as someone who has made a career of it. They have written more words and been through the quality control ringer, over and over, and now they're a better author. Your standard is you. Your first foray is a starting point for improvement to get to a place where you can be proud of your own work. You are what you create.

Chapter 3 – Can You Believe It? There's More.

YOU WEAR TWO HATS—AN *Artist Hat and a Business Hat*

Sometimes you need to be the talent, nurtured with chocolate and blankets on a cold day. Other times, you need to put on your suit and tie and slam the gavel, demanding the talent to come clean on when they're going to finish the current book. You can't sell what you don't have, and you have fans who are hungry for the books. Don't let them starve! If you're smart enough to write the book, you're smart enough to run an author business.

Don't Waste Time Drinking Bad Beer

I don't drink to excess anymore. I might have one beer a month. Because of that, it reinforces my point that more isn't better. Only better is better. Don't waste that one beer drinking a bad one. Only you know if you are able to produce more through better writing habits, better preparation, better efforts at removing distractions. You are in control of your business. Too many think they're creating when they're actually doofing off. Get to work. Do the work. You'll find that better is better and you can produce an awful lot if you are committed to it. More and better is best.

Self-publishing Is a Learning Journey

Don't expect to be great at it on your first attempt. It takes time to learn all the things. If you try to learn all the things before you do the things, then the things will be ephemeral, vanishing like will-o'-the-wisps in a swamp. There's nothing like muscle memory to make your second, third, and later publications better. From writing to publishing to marketing. It gets easier the more you do it, which applies to just about everything in life.

Time Is the Currency of Your Life

Measure your business in the time it takes to do the things that must be done. Allocate your time as you would spend money. How much time of actual writing does it take to produce a book? Eighty hours? Two hundred hours? It doesn't matter what the answer is, but work that into your time checkbook and keep track. It makes forecasting easier and better. It helps you manage your business through allocating time.

Master the Process

The ones who understand and control the process of writing and publishing a book will benefit the most. Control what's in your control. If you're smart enough to write the book, you're smart enough to do everything else that needs to be done. You don't have to like it, you only have to do it. Then master it for maximum benefits while investing the greatest amount of energy in the writing of great stories.

Plan Ahead

From knowing what you want to say in the next paragraph to knowing the book you want to write twelve months down the road. Even a loose plan is better than no plan. I put together a list at the beginning of the year for the books I want to write. I list them, prioritize them, and then make them happen. One or two may drop out, but the majority get done. I think about them early and when I finally put pen to paper, I know where the story is going.

Balance Writing with Marketing

You can't sell a product you don't have. As a full-time author, more than half of my time is spent writing the next book. A robust backlist is important to overall business health. It can help you overcome a new series that doesn't take off. With a little extra focus on marketing, you can pick up sales that give you time and money to keep writing. At the initial start of your career, it's important to get those words, improve your writing, and build a backlist.

The Only Limits in the Business Are the Ones You Put on Yourself

The greatest limiting factor is what we do to ourselves. You have to be willing to study your craft, read, write, learn, and then do all that business stuff it takes when you're an entrepreneur. And you can do it, you just need to stop blocking yourself. Set a goal and take the steps necessary to reach it.

Marketing Is a Necessary Evil

There's no magic that will pick up your book and carry it away. You have to tell people that it's there. It starts with you, unless you have a lot of extra money you don't mind throwing away to pay someone else to sell your book baby. I don't advise that. You can do the marketing without the horrible "Buy my book" approach. It's a process where if you put yourself into your optimal reader's mind, you can see what catches their eye. Do that with your book.

Characters Move Your Plot Forward

Many recent Hollywood movies have lost sight of this fact. CGI is cool, special effects blow us away, but the characters are what we keep coming back for. Are yours relatable, consistent, flawed but growing? The plot is the backbone, but the characters are the flesh and blood of your story. Bring them to life within the readers' minds.

Get Out of Your Box

You can't learn if you don't look beyond your own small world. There's a lot out there. See what you can see, learn what there is to learn, and you'll find that there is always something more to discover. This is what will make you a great writer. Stretch your wings and fly.

Bad Reviews

They are a badge of honor, and they're also an opportunity to learn. Everyone gets bad reviews because there are a lot of unhappy people in the world. Sometimes, it's because they feel betrayed that what they thought they were buying wasn't what the story turned out to be. Sometimes, they want to show the author that they're smarter. Don't measure your worth against people who are unhappy and willing to share their angst to drag you down. Shared misery doesn't make anyone feel better. Stay above the noise. Be kind in all things. Their battles aren't your battles. And then work to refine your target audience toward the types of people who gave your book favorable reviews. More of them and less of the former.

Where Does Growth Happen?

Outside your comfort zone. It may be a cliché, but that's because it is right a lot more often than it's wrong. How far outside your comfort zone? Don't be a lunatic. Stretch your boundaries and enlarge your comfort zone. Don't move to a whole different time zone and set up shop. That is an added level of stress that you probably don't need.

Drama

Sometimes, you don't have to express an opinion about an issue that's going on out in the real world. All social media is a cesspool of emotional engagement. That's how they make their money. It's what people with too much time on their hands do—gossip around the water cooler. It doesn't matter what others do. Look at yourself and what you need to accomplish in your author career. Invest your time in that.

Begin with the End in Mind

It's easier to plan your way ahead if you can put yourself at your destination and visualize the steps it took to get there. Being a wildly successful (and rich) author takes a great deal of effort that's in your control, but also much that isn't in your control. You have no dominion over sales, the easiest metric to gauge success. However, you can create the conditions for increasing sales by writing better and better books, using well-targeted marketing, and growing your readership foundation.

Authoring Is Not a Zero-Sum Game

You don't have to lose for me to win. We can all win together, because readers can read far more than we can write. Helping readers find good quality books to read in between our releases is a great service that we can provide. "My favorite author recommended..." Write a great book. Be the person others recommend and then take the time to recommend others to your readership. We all win together.

Being a Professional Author

Have you sold your books? Congratulations. You're a professional author. It's a low bar, but that's all it takes. Have you sold your books to strangers? Have you snagged a #1 New Release tag from Amazon or even better, a "Bestseller" banner? Take a screenshot so you can always carry that with you.

You Decide the Day You Want to Have

It starts when you get up from sleeping. Are you ready for the day? Even if you're not, you still get to choose. You have things to do. You have to work. You have a sick child. You can lament your lot in life, or you can get after it. Do the things. Put yourself into a better place mentally. Only you can do that. It would be nice if your kids thanked you for wiping their snotty noses, but they probably won't until much later in life when you realize they've turned into good people. The more you're miserable, the more you exude that to everyone you meet. The more you're happy, the more people will enjoy being around you.

You are Who You're Surrounded By

In professional circles, there are organizations for the top performers. Davos, Switzerland, for those with the greatest financial portfolios. Like-minded people, hanging out together to stay at the top of their game. As an author, you have an unprecedented opportunity to spend time with some of the greatest authors of our generation. They go to some big conferences and when there, they are generally available. They'll talk to small groups. Buy them a beverage and enjoy a few minutes of their time. Be kind in all things and you'll see that reflected in more renowned authors inviting you to more and more events. Don't be a straphanger. Be a player. Work hard at the right things.

The Value of Author Peers

Once you realize that your peers are far more successful than you as well as not as successful, you'll be in a better mental state to engage with them. Don't ever talk down to another author, no matter where you think they are on some arbitrary scale of importance. We create alone, but we're authors together. Maybe it's shared misery because authoring is hard. Maybe it's just a shared journey that we're on together to entertain and educate the readers. You're not alone. Enjoy the company of your peers. They know what you're going through and vice versa.

One Person

The power of one to build. The power of one to destroy. Be the one who changes other's lives for the better. It starts with you. Because it's not just one person you can influence by your example. I'm not talking about leaning on a Ferrari pitching snake oil. I'm talking about hope. It keeps us going when all else fails. Hope that we too can improve our lives.

Celebrate Your Victories

If you want awards and you earn those, celebrate them. If you want to make a living and are, celebrate that. If you are increasing your revenue year over year, celebrate that. Create your action plan, work toward your goals, and get it done. Your journey is yours alone. Mine is mine.

The Reader Experience

It is both subjective and objective. You can measure it in your reader recidivism. What's your read-through rate to the next title? Are you getting good numbers of reviews? More than before with each new release? Is your book ranking better than it should be based on sales alone? Those are all signs of a positive reader experience.

Chapter 4 – In Case You Didn't Get Enough Earlier, Even More Stuff

ADD ALL FIVE SENSES for Better Emotional Engagement

That's right—smell, touch, sounds, and taste add to the emotional experience. Can you taste that tequila you had in college? What kind of reaction does it invoke? Jaeger bombs... Senses turn a scene into a three-dimensional experience. Try it and see how you can bring your characters and scenes to life.

To Change Your Life, You Have to Change Your Circumstances

That seems like a simple axiom, but change is hard, like really freaking hard. We settle into a pattern and stick with it because it's comfortable, even if it's not best for us. What do you want out of life? Take that goal and look backward from there until today. See the steps in between? There are probably a lot, but it only takes that first step. Write the first paragraph of your book and hold onto it tightly as you expand and grow your story. Do something different today that will help you reach your goal of tomorrow.

Are You Happy?

This is a question that you need to ask yourself fairly often. It could take years of building your author business before you can honestly say that you are happy as an author. Will it take a huge number of sales? Possibly. We only want our work to be appreciated. If you have a small but vocal group of fans, find out what makes them tick. Then market to more readers just like them. Your happiness goal will change as you progress through your career. At first, you'll be happy when you get that book written. Then you'll be happy with that first sale. Then it'll take the first million page reads. The goalposts keep moving, and that's the reality of life. Ask yourself the question often, making sure you look back to see how far you've come.

Look Back Every Now and Then

You have to see how far you've come to appreciate that the light in the distance is closer. You may never reach that far point, but you'll have been on a journey worthy of a book or three. Even writing your first book. Look at that! It started with the first word, and now it's taking shape. The characters have been brought to life and they're doing what we can relate to. They are living a life we can live with them.

This May be Small Potatoes to Some...

Don't ever demean yourself by comparing yourself to others, not when it comes to authoring. You can only compare your journey to your journey.

Measure how far *you've* come. That's what matters. Announce your little victories as big victories. We'll cheer together. All that matters is you're doing better today than yesterday, this year over the last. Keep moving forward. No potatoes are small, so don't be an absolute potato. No matter how big you are, there will always be someone bigger. No matter how small you are, there will always be that person who said they wanted to write a book but never did and never will. Don't be that guy. Those are big potatoes.

Manage Your Readers' Expectations

You can build a readership that defies seasonal norms. You can deliver books one month apart or one year apart. All you have to do is let your readers know. They don't like surprises, so don't surprise them. Keep them informed by keeping your commitments. Give yourself the opportunity to make every self-imposed deadline. If you keep missing target dates that you yourself have committed to, then the readers will stop trusting you and move on to authors they know will deliver when they say.

The Routine of Long-term Authordom

You wake up. You get your coffee or tea or Diet Coke and think of the words waiting to be written while drifting back to the words already there, fiddling with them to make them better. And then you flow into the blank page. It's as simple as that. Whether the thinking happens in your sleep or waiting for the kids to finish school or on a lunch break, the thinking and then the writing. It's so much easier to write if you know what you want to say.

Passion

There's a lot to be said for writing with passion. That is something I see in my earlier books. Although they aren't as complex as newer stories, they flow well and keep the reader reading. A stream of consciousness that stays on target. It's not rambling. It's writing down what you see from the world you've created, and you're doing it as fast as you can type. Don't lose the wary eye of creation.

Learn What You Need to Know, When You Need to Know It

There is far too much to know in self-publishing to know it all before you publish your first work. Merchandise? Don't waste time with that until you're ready to sell merchandise. You can easily get overwhelmed if you try to learn it all before you press the "publish" button. Just work the problems one at a time, starting with getting the book out there, then getting it into the right readers' hands. One bowling pin at a time until they're all knocked down. Don't bend under immense pressure. One small step at a time will get you where you want to go.

If You Keep Rewriting the Same Book, You'll Have Only Written One Book

The learning value in crossing the same ground over and over, again and again, is extremely limited. You learn nothing about the publishing process. You don't grow as an author, because there's no progression. There's no input from strangers, neither acceptance nor rejection. Nothing. Publish, learn, grow, repeat.

The Glory of Authordom

If you're in this business for the glory, you're going to be disappointed far more than not. We're like fireworks with our moments of eye-popping bliss followed by weeks of cold preparation in between joyful explosions of color and sound painted across the sky. There isn't much of that at all. Authoring is hard work. It's especially taxing mentally. Sometimes, the greatest glory is in getting a good night's sleep after a long day of writing.

The Trial of Success

Once you've published and start to realize a modicum of success, you'll find that some of your friends will change. Some may want stuff from you. Some may vilify your success, but passively. And some may drift away as you gain new friends in your new profession—even if nothing else has changed. This may seem dark, but it is the harsh reality of success in a public forum. Take care and understand that success may not change you, but it very well could change those around you. And it could change you, too, but that's within your control.

No One Gets Out Alive

Keep your author affairs in order, just in case. Your legacy depends on it, even if you only have one book. That will go on forever, but will you relegate it to a forgotten corner of the internet, or will you keep things sorted in a way that gives your heirs a way to keep your legacy alive? It's up to you. Start today.

The Value of Free

Giving a book away for free carries some risk. What if they take it and never read it? Then you'll get no sales on the next book. What if they don't take it, not even for free? That might be a blow to your ego. It also suggests there might be an alignment issue between the cover and the blurb where the readers aren't excited about the book. And then there's the rest of the time where someone finds the free book interesting enough to start reading. It is well written, so they keep reading and then buy the next books in the series. Also, if your book is on Amazon and in Kindle Unlimited, the "Read for Free" button is huge, and many readers click on that instead of the "Buy for $0.00." You win.

Get Out of Your Own Way

Sometimes the greatest obstacle between you and your success is you. Recognize when you're holding yourself back, because it won't be anything that you can directly put your finger on. You'll dither about because it's not perfect and you have high standards. That's a bunch of bullshit. You're afraid of being called a clown. Guess what? Mean people will call you names anyway, not because you're a clown but because they're mean. More people will probably like your story if it fits with most genre tropes and delivers a great reader experience. Remember, there's no such thing as perfect.

Chapter 5 – Beyond Stuff

You Are Your Brand

Once you publish, you become the ambassador of your brand. It's doubtful you'll only write one series in a single genre. Once you start writing, you find that you've fertilized the idea factory and you're going to run out of time before you run out of stories. Be your brand—yourself, but the good side of yourself. As an author, you can be whatever you want to be. Live life through your characters or as the overseer of the characters' misadventures. Have fun with it, but don't lose your way. Once you've gained a fan, try to keep them on board.

Dress for the Job You Want

Being your brand is a great thing. You want to be a great sci-fi author? What's stopping you? Strap on your laser pistol and magnetic boots and go to town! If you can be Batman, always be Batman. I worked too many years in the corporate world. If I wanted the next job in the hierarchy, I had to act like I was already there, from clothing to demeanor to ability. You want to be like a best-selling author? Then get covers from whoever designs those perpetually at the top. Do what the successful do. Establish a mindset that helps you take the steps to reach your goal.

Nothing Sells the Last Book Like the Next Book

Readers want to know you aren't going to leave them hanging. If they enjoy your writing, they'll want more. Period. Give it to them. The more you write, the better you get at writing. The more you build a fanbase jonesing for the next book, the more lucrative your career will be.

It's Easier to Sell Ten Books to One Person than One Book to Ten Different People

So much easier. Write a great book. Then write the next one even better. That first book will lead to buy-through, also read-through for subscription services. That's where your high-priced advertising pays off. Lead the readers from one book to the next by including links in your back matter, right after The End. Send them to that next book. It's pure profit when the readers keep reading.

Genre Equals Marketing

All genre (or categories, BISAC codes) do is provide a stable of readers who like particular types of books. From tropes to settings to themes, genre has been the landing zone where marketing takes place. If the reader liked book alpha because it talked about dragons, then the reader might like book bravo because it also has dragons. That's all genre is. I recommend you find the largest pool of readers who might like your book. Don't niche yourself into obscurity.

Life-changing Money

Know what your life-changing money figure is and strive for it. Include your expenses, current and future. Understand your profit margin. Being an author entrepreneur is a little more than writing a great story. Manage your business to realize the fruits of your labors.

If You're Smart Enough to Write a Book, You're Smart Enough to Do All the Other Stuff, Too

Writing a book is the hardest part. If you can manage that, you can handle the rest of it. Income and expenses, services, and marketing. It all flows together to put your book into the right readers' hands. You don't have to love all the other stuff. You only have to do it. Love the writing, tolerate the rest, but learn it so you can teach someone else to do it for you. The cycle is complete when you can do nothing but write and oversee the other processes.

Unsolicited Advice is Criticism

As authors, we're always looking to tighten up the written word, help make sentences clearer. If we do this for someone who didn't ask for it, you could crush their soul. You're criticizing, not helping. Let them go unless they ask for help, then make sure to define the parameters of your assistance.

Don't Reincarnate as a Human

If you keep doing the same thing over and over, you'll get the same result. Try being a goat or maybe a salamander. Imagine what you'll learn seeing the world through their eyes. Explore greater boundaries with your writing. Look through a different lens.

Is This a Business or a Hobby?

Decide early and don't hedge. If you want to be a professional, then you have to put your books in front of strangers. You have to weather the criticism, even if it's a storm. And then you have to do it again and again. If you keep calling yourself a hobby writer hoping that you start making money, you're sabotaging yourself. In Yoda's immortal words, do or do not. Don't lie to yourself. If you want to be a successful professional author, then make the commitment and do the work.

Make Your Own Luck

In the author business as well as any business, if you're counting on luck, then you better stack the deck by working hard at those things that are important to the business. As an author, it's writing a great story. It's finding the right readers by marketing to those places where they are looking, and it's getting them interested in the book and keeping them interested because they love what they read.

Writing a Book Is the Hardest Thing You'll Ever Do

When you're finished writing it, you'll find out it's only half the battle. But that's okay. When you've finished, you will always be able to embrace how you brought your imagination and thoughts to paper. Selling it is a different issue, but don't forget to look back through your writing process to see what worked, what didn't, and feel the joy of having a finished book.

A Trope Helps You Align with Your Target Readership

Genre equals marketing. In that vein, you need to understand what the readers are expecting. If you're not aligned, then your book may have problems. This is why it's important to read in the genre you write. Know what the tropes are. Stick with ninety percent and save the extra ten percent to add your own flare. Don't lose your readers before you bring them on board.

Time Is the Currency of Your Business

Everything comes down to time. Do you have what you need to finish what needs to be finished? Invest your time as you do your money. Allocate the resources necessary while understanding your limitations. Don't commit to a hundred-hour project when you only have ten hours available. This seems simple, but it's not. It's hard saying 'no' to others, saying 'no' to our own whims. Time is a finite resource. Once wasted, you cannot get it back.

Time, Part Deux

You pay with your time as that becomes money, and money buys the things you don't have time to learn or can't produce for yourself. I buy covers because learning to do them is not something I am equipped for. I don't have time to learn a new trade. I'll invest mine in what I'm good at—writing a story.

Leveling Up

The most successful money-earning authors have a healthy backlist of good books that readers love. The fewer books you have, the more marketing you must do to make a positive return on investment (ROI). If you're able to make money on few books because you've honed your marketing chops, you'll do very well when you have more books. There's the rub. If you spend your time learning marketing, then you aren't writing extra books to bolster your backlist. That means, it all takes time.

The Freedom to Be and Your Legacy

In a hundred years, few of us will be remembered, but our books will still be available. Of this, I have no doubt. Digital storage is available, and our works are in libraries and library collections, searchable and findable. Looking through the lens of tomorrow is the best way to see today. How will history see you? Create the history of your future by doing the right things now. Arguing on Facebook? Being unkind to other authors? Maybe that makes you feel better today, but I doubt it. You lose your spark, and eternity leaves you behind. Sounds like a lose-lose. Write great books and tell the stories that are untold. Build your legacy.

The Future of Ideas is Now

What are you working on? Is it the best idea you've had yet for characters and plot? Those are the foundation of all great stories. Characters that your readers can relate to doing things that your readers revel in watching them do. Or revel in imagining themselves there, doing great things. Being great. Escaping today. The readers can't escape if your story isn't out there for them.

Don't Spend Your Windfall Incurring More Debt

What happens when you have that great month? Finance a new house and a new car! I suggest you don't do that because you'll have to earn that much every month and in this business, there are ups *and* downs. If you can pay down your debt or buy something you need for cash, go for it. I also recommend banking some of your windfall for a rainy day. Make sure you have enough to pay your monthly expenses for three months. That gives you breathing room in a downturn.

Never Too Old

You're never too old to write, and a book is never too old to promote. I started writing full time after I turned 52. You're never too old or decrepit to weave a great story. I submit to you that your age and experience will help tell better tales with more realism and greater character depth because you're speaking from a lifetime of experience. Maybe it's too late for that professional football career, but it's not too late to be an author. And that old book of yours? It's not too late for that to find new readers, either.

Making It

Not everyone will, but that's because some set their sights too high, and others don't set their sights at all. Still more aren't doing what they need to make it. You must ask yourself, what does it mean to "make it?" It starts with writing that first book, completing it, and seeing it for sale where strangers can buy and read it. That's the first hurdle over which all authors must pass. And your story is good, but not great. What does it take to make the book great? Rewriting the same story or moving to the next? Are you going to rerun the same race, or are you going to stretch your legs, train, and help your mind to dominate the obstacles before you?

Churn the Words! Get that Book Out There!

These are siren cries that have been mangled from an original premise that was to write the best book you can as quickly as you can. If you publish garbage, that is where it will end up—the trash heap of history. You have to write a good story in a great way. You have to embroil the reader in the thoughts you've created within their minds. This is not to say that writing fast makes for bad books or writing slowly makes for good books. Writing a good book is what makes for a good book, whatever your process and speed.

Is Your Book Good Enough?

Cue imposter syndrome, second-guessing, claims of "being a perfectionist." Just because you're paranoid doesn't mean someone's not out to get you. Maybe your book isn't good enough. There are over ten million books available on Amazon. That's eleventy billion different ways someone can seek entertainment that's something other than your book. What are you doing to sharpen how you deliver the images in your mind through the words on the page to the minds of the readers? That is what you do as an author.

Chapter 6 – Son of Stuff

REVENUE FOLLOWS YOUR HABITS

Masters of the process will set themselves up for success. Building good habits to write, to review, to market, to order covers early, to publish when ready, and more. Develop good habits that support a professional author career, whether you write full time or not.

You Can't Sell a Book You Haven't Written

The best of intentions won't give you a sellable product. You have to write the book. An idea is nothing more than a dream without putting it on paper (or into your computer). This is why ideas alone can't be copyrighted. You have to write it.

Turning the idea into a manuscript is what gets copyrighted.

Butt in Chair, Hands on Keyboard

The best habit you can develop as an author is the love of writing, even when you don't feel like it. Get the words. Reap the rewards.

Think Before You Write

It goes so much faster if you know what you want to say. Whether it's a scene setup, the action, a transition, a description, dialogue, it doesn't matter. Take two minutes to think through the next paragraph or the next page before you start typing. You can produce more quickly rather than writing without using your brain. Plus, it'll be better. Your fingers don't know the story.

What Drives Your Main Character(s)?

Always keep that at the forefront of your mind. The character's motivation helps you be consistent in your story and if you start getting stuck, you can always look back at the motivation and stay true to that. Each character in their own time. Each character trying to improve.

Explore Your Boundaries

Unless you try, you don't know what you're capable of. Test yourself. Even if you've gotten older and can't do what you used to, you can still do something. What are your boundaries? You don't know until you know.

What Is the Value of Your Time?

Don't sell yourself short. A quality hour of writing time can be worth hundreds or even thousands of dollars. Because a quality hour isn't paid over one hour. It's paid out over all the years your story is out there, with readers buying it and enjoying it. Your value per hour only increases over time.

Kindle Unlimited (KU) Payout Pool

If you have your books in Kindle Direct Publishing Select (Kindle Unlimited for the readers), then it's best if you consider yourself a shareholder in Amazon overall. KU fortunes are tied to how well Amazon does during the month, and that is the entire site, not just the KU payout pool. The pool goes up and the rate per page read goes down. No one is ripping you off. There is a hard bottom that has only been crossed once. Generally, you'll see at least $0.004 (four tenths of a cent) per page read in the KU program. You want the readers to start reading and keep reading. That's what gets you paid.

Vengeance Against Authors Who Have Wronged You

Cut that crap out. Going to war with other authors is a lose-lose proposition. Ignore and move on. Build your brand with your readers. That relationship will carry you through. There are trolls, scumbags, and toxic personalities in every profession. The professional author world is no different. Let them scream into the void. Let them throw their vile word daggers at anyone and everyone. Feel pity for them. You're better than that. Be a professional.

Learn from Your Mistakes

How can you grow if you don't learn? Life is a learning journey. You will make mistakes. Learn from them and move on. Don't let them define the real you. Don't make the same mistake over and over. That is a rut from which you'll never escape.

The Three Pillars of Marketing

Brand, advertising, and promotions. Long-term is your brand. Always release the best book you can, keeping in mind there's no such thing as perfect. Advertising is short-term to put your books in front of new readers. Ads appeal to an instant gratification audience. Promotions get the widest visibility for your titles in a short time. These are your paid newsletters, shared newsletters, and broad-based readership engagement. In the end, brand is what will extend your author career. Readers come on board because of an ad or a promotion, but they stay because they like your writing style, stories, and characters.

Positive Reinforcement

Reward the behavior you want to see more of. When people help you, the least you can do is say thank you. The same goes for yourself. How do you reward yourself for doing the right things in your author business? What do you do when you finish that first draft? What do you do after you've set up a solid marketing campaign? Reward and learn. Treat yourself to something nice that you only get with completion.

The Author Race—Hustle!

Is this how you feel? Are you under pressure? (Cue Freddie and David.) The only race you're a part of is a marathon, and you're the only contestant. Here's a secret. So many people. So much success! You find your own way. Pushing harder doesn't work. It only annoys the people around you, packs the crowd more tightly in front of you, and sends your stress to heart attack levels. Don't do that to yourself. Work at a pace that fits you, while exploring your boundaries. Writing one book a year when you know you can write four without any problem isn't going to do your business any favors, but writing four books when your body and situation—day job, young kids—suggest you should only write one won't do you any favors, either.

Help Those Who Help Themselves

Once you've reached some level of success, you'll get requests from newer authors for assistance, advice, and all manner of things. My first rule is to find out what they are doing for themselves. Flailing is not an action plan. Studying the business is. I wrote a book, now what do I do? It's a valid question, but there are a number of Facebook groups, Discord channels, and YouTubers who are more than happy to share what's next at no cost. Sometimes people want the shortcut. I'm not doing that for new authors because there's a certain amount of understanding that is behind why I do what I do. Without some shared experience, we're not speaking the same language. Climb in the trenches and see the world from there.

This Is Not an Easy Business

There's a small percentage of authors making the majority of the money. BUT! Big but. That club is not exclusive based on birthright, Wall Street connections, political affiliation, or anything besides their ability to reach readers. That is as low a bar as exists in a capitalist world. You reap the rewards therefrom. You personally benefit from your labors. You write the book readers want to read. And then write another. The mid-list authors, those earning (net, not gross) more than six figures a year, are a huge club. Amazon says there are a thousand. I think there are a lot more than that.

Find Your Tribe

The power in being an author is your peers. No writer is better or worse. There are only those with more experience. Find those of your like mindset, genre, and aspirations. You'll discover that you have a great deal in common. Differences are limited to scope of vision and translating that to the written word. Experience. Being a writer is about writing. Share that aspect with others of similar ilk and you'll find a whole new way of looking at an author career.

Are You Still Having Fun?

Never forget why you started writing, You are the talent. You are the imagination come to life. You are the reason you're writing. Hold onto that. Have fun writing. If you go full time, you're counting on the revenue from book sales to keep a roof over your head and food on your table, but when you stop having fun, it becomes a painful grind. Seek the joy in writing and your readers will reward you.

Review Your Business

If for no other reason than to see how far you've come and that the business side of being an author isn't scary. Business is nothing to be feared. It's a simple spreadsheet or list of numbers and dates and contact information that is managed month to month. Are you getting the most from the money you're spending? That's what every business has to do, whether it's a trillion-dollar corporation or a single author's sole proprietorship. See yourself as a business and excel.

Self-discipline Is Self-control

Know your goals and continue to march toward them. If you find yourself getting distracted, then your self-discipline is waning. Get yourself under control and back on track. It is as simple as that. Don't let shiny-thing syndrome pull you away from having a successful author career. Each time you get distracted, you deviate from your goal. You are in control of how you invest your time. Don't give that up for anything. Stay on target.

It helped Luke Skywalker defeat the Empire. It'll help you.

There's Nothing Better than Being an Author

I can say that over and over and it never gets old. I've had a number of careers, and nothing comes close to being an author. Those other things? They gave me fodder for my novels, an endless supply of people and situations to weave into my stories. And then I do it again but better.

Are You Ready to Live Your Dream?

Did you do the work it takes? We don't always get what we want. Sometimes the work is too hard, and obstacles block our way. Are you determined to work hard at the right things? It means to fill the gaps in the foundation of your small business, to make it function like a real business, starting with a product that can sell.

Write the Best Book You Can

It's all anyone can do, as long as you understand that you'll get better as you go. Your first attempt at writing a book may not be very good in the big scheme of things, but it's going to be the best you could do at the time. Practicing is how you get better, which means writing more than one book.

There's No Glass Ceiling

Even if you have to bootstrap it, never spending more than you make, you can do that. It might take a little longer, but it can be done. Use your mind and hold your panic at bay. It has no place in this business. Put your self-defeating behaviors in a timeout and keep them there. You know exactly what they are. We all have them. But we're in control here. This isn't fourth and goal with the ball snapped. You don't have to make any decisions with only two seconds to think about it. You can manage your business better than that.

The Quality of a Good Story

You can always sell a good book, whether through different packaging or better audience targeting. When talking craft, what works for one doesn't necessarily work for all. Different genres demand different tropes demand different stories. For a career, quality is critical. But quality can be summed up in a simple phrase. "Good enough to entertain the reader and make them come back for more." That is the quality standard that matters. You can publish a bad book. No error is fatal. Just unpublish it or rewrite it, take your lessons, move on. Get better. Write more. Practice until your baseline is well above the "good enough to keep the readers coming back" standard.

Chapter 7– Grandpuppy of Stuff

WHO ARE YOU?

As an author, you get to be what you wish. Become the person your readers look up to. Leave your baggage in the past and develop a persona that is glorious! A person of honor and pride, one to be respected. That means respecting your readers and standing tall without looking down on others. Lift people up around you and watch yourself rise.

Aerogonomics

That's ergonomics with some aerobics thrown in for good measure. Is your writing space optimized for your body? If you spend any amount of time writing, you'll want to buy a good chair and a table that fits with it so you can avoid any pain or injuries related to long-term discomfort and misalignment. A comfortable body delivers better prose from a mind that's free to focus instead of being distracted by the noise of anguish. Work smarter, not harder.

The Power of Positivity

We can see the rain or the rainbow. Unless you're in the UK, then it's just more rain, but that's why there are bumbershoots and slickers. I jest, because some things must be laughed at. You control how you respond to things. Toxic people, even if they're family. You have to deal with them. Remove their toxicity from your existence. Sometimes, all you need is a kind word to lift your head out of the doom swamp. The more you're positive toward others, the more you'll find that people will be positive toward you.

The Race of Self-Publishing

The race is run only against yourself. What are you capable of doing? Do it a little better today than yesterday—as in those things within your control that you are trying to improve. Clean up those crutch words. Kill the run-on sentences before they run on. Smooth the prose, tighten the transitions, make the action more three-dimensional. And real. Write better and you'll write faster. But never forget that the race is against yourself, no one else.

The Lesson of Elvis

What I saw in Graceland was an epically unhappy artistic genius who lost control of his own life and ended up dying from a prescription drug overdose at 42. Here are the life lessons I took away from that. 1: No one is responsible for your success but you. Others may help, but they have no claim on your words. 2: The more successful you are, the more "friends" who will appear in your life. Be wary. 3: If you want to eat a chili dog and a fried peanut butter and banana sandwich, eat it. 4: Buying toys will not make you happy when what you really need is peace of mind.

What's a Launch Strategy When You Have No Books Published?

From a strategic perspective, you don't know how your book will be received, you probably aren't sure of the exact genre (for marketing purposes), you aren't sure of the technical process of publishing. So many things that you don't know, but there is one simple way to get some of that information—publish your book. You don't have to build a readership before you have anything for them to read. You don't have to set up blog tours or promotions. You don't have to do any of that. It takes bait to attract the fish. No one dangles a bare hook and expects to catch anything. With a product, you now have the means to attract readers, those people who might like your style and read your books.

Writing to Market

Writing with a target audience in mind is nothing more than writing your own great story in a genre that you read (so you understand what other readers of that type of book expect). Selling our art is how we feed ourselves and our family. That's not mercenary. That's life. Doing it right means you get to buy vegetables at the farmer's market versus spending less at a grocery store to buy lesser quality that's on sale. Why do you deserve a lesser life?

The Allure of Tomorrow

Live for today. Plan for tomorrow. Don't let worries about tomorrow rob you of today's joy. Tomorrow is the dream you haven't realized. Embrace the hope that is a new day, today, so you can live your best life both today and tomorrow.

Networking

An author is alone with their computer, creating and writing. But they aren't alone, not in the world of today where we can be instantaneously connected across twenty-four time zones. As an author, understand that your peers are every other author. We win together.

Talking to Real People, in Person

Screw that. Write more books.

Dialogue Drives Relations

When your characters speak, they come to life, especially with those whom they interact with. Dialogue shows more about them than any kind of third person omni exposition or inner thoughts. If you can show them in dialogue rather than telling through narrative, your scenes and characters will be more vibrant. People are judged by their actions, not their intentions.

The Less Often You Publish, the More You Have to Market

There are benefits to being prolific. You keep your readers on the hook and ready to receive that next book. If you write one or two books a year, you have to fill the time in between with marketing to keep the revenue flowing. Nothing sells the last book like the next book. Get that next book written, cleaned up, and published. You still have to market, but not as much when you deliver a steady supply of new titles to your growing readership.

You Have to Sell Your Soul for a Good Story

I'm kidding. There is no soul-selling needed. A good story is simply a bunch of what-ifs that lead you through a tale. Give your story a plot for a backbone with a couple inspired ideas and characters that are fun and that the readers can relate to. Voila! You have a story. At some point in time, you will be someone's favorite author.

The Difference Between Author Expectations and Reader Experience

You're probably the worst judge of your books. From self-induced anxiety based on the fear of rejection all the way to thinking you're the greatest author who ever lived. You're all wrong. The readers are the ones who judge. Those buying your books and then those convincing others to buy your books. From the depths of obscurity to a viral sensation. Robert E. Howard killed himself at the age of thirty after writing a vast collection of stories that saw little success during his lifetime. A tortured artist. Until Conan became one of the most popular franchises in history.

The Business of Being a Self-published Author

It's your business. It's all you and your capital to move it forward. It's all you and your personality to make a connection with your readers. It's all you to write the books that people want to read. It can be a lonely business. You'll spend a great deal of time by yourself, in your own mind, creating the story and using your words to bring it to life. This isn't a sprint, not by any stretch of the imagination. It's a slog, and the crater-filled road is lined with notebooks and pens of wannabe authors. It's like getting a PhD. You have to stick it out. Why hold yourself to lesser standards than other professionals?

You Bear the Risk and Reap All the Rewards

The risk is the investment of your time and maybe some money, but you can spend almost nothing until you have your product completed. Then you can test the market. Will strangers like your book? They may. You are probably the worst judge of that, so now you start a new phase of the product life cycle. Defining the market and determining product placement. It's not insurmountable. It's one of the coolest things you'll do in your life.

There are Times When the World Can Be Overwhelming

The kindness of strangers. The warm embrace of a community of professionals who are more like family. The sharing of wisdom learned the hard way, through experiences both good and bad. You are responsible for your own success, but none of us can go it alone. The world can be a harsh place when there's no one to lean on, share your trials with, celebrate your successes. Leave the drama of a gray and unhappy world behind. You may have to walk through a briar patch or three on your way to find the end of the rainbow, but look at all the great things you'll see along the way! Some say it's not the destination but the journey that matters. How many times have your goals changed based on what you learned as you went?

Changing the World, One Person at a Time

Because we can all rise together on a tide of our own making. For those who are authoring for the right reasons, doing the hard work in the right way, learning, improving, striving to create better and better books. For our readers. For our families. For our legacy.

The Fallacy of Now

Everyone is on a different journey. I could not start mine until I was 52, after I had retired from two previous careers. I had a solid financial support system in place as I started writing full-time, having never written a book before. But I knew I wouldn't fail. I had three ideas for stories, so I wrote all three. Now, I have more ideas than I can write.

Passive Income

Writing? If you ever hear someone refer to being an author as a source of passive income, have a good laugh and then get back to work. There's nothing passive about being an author. If you stop everything you're doing, your sales will taper off to zero. You keep writing, keep promoting, and keep moving forward.

Author Professionals

There is no debate between authors about whose books are crap and whose aren't. Those are stupid arguments between petty and bitter people. Those are people who want to be full-time authors but will never be because they haven't gotten "lucky." Tearing someone else down never made you a better writer or, more importantly, more engaging with your fans.

Inspiration

I need to dispel any kind of myth that you should only write when inspired. You should get story ideas down when inspired. The rest of the time, you have to have a workmanlike attitude in creating the scenes and weaving them together. It's a lot of perspiration in between those moments of inspiration.

Realizing Success

Your chances of realizing success are orders of magnitude greater than what they were twenty years ago, specifically because of quality author groups where you can learn and grow. I think we're the best when it comes to the business of being a self-published author. We aren't going to help you write your stories better, but when you have a story that's good enough, come in here and browse the buffet of what's next. You're sitting on the first brick in the foundation of your writing career. Your author peers know a bit about the business and are sharing that knowledge.

The Sanctity of Fear

We are conditioned to avoid risks, and even those who get a thrill from X games talk about how it makes their blood pump. That's their bodies telling them to be afraid. Courage is addressing your fear. As authors, our fears are less physical and more mental. Will readers like my book? Will I spend more than I make? When is that one-star review coming? What if my cover artist bails on me and takes my money? My editor is changing my voice! Address your fears, one at a time, and accept that you will never be completely free of them. This will keep you both humble and alert.

Write the Next Book

There is power in your backlist, having a robust catalogue. Write with intentionality – for a target audience, building on previous work, in a genre that you love to read. Write each new paragraph better than the one before. Write stories that people want to read. Build on your success, even if you have to start over.

Quantity Has a Quality All Its Own (part deux)

It helps to have a variety of titles for readers to pick up once they find you. It also helps for that work to be the best you can make it, without overdoing your self-defeating tendency toward an ethereal "perfection." More isn't necessarily better, only better is better. But more of better is best.

Chapter 8–
Deputy
Undersecretary
of Stuff

Hobbies

If you do what you love, you never work a day in your life! That's an oft trotted out phrase that belies the work of being an author who loves to write. As an author, you'll work every single day of your life. Even if not writing, you'll be thinking about the stories or promotions or cover art. Your mind won't take a break unless you force it to by engaging in your hobbies. Don't leave those behind when begin your author career. It's important to give your mind a break and do something completely different.

Fear of a Bad Review

No. Stop that madness. It's not failure. You sold a book! Realizing value from your words is part of the business of being an author and publisher. Business isn't easy, but it's not hard, either. Don't be your own enemy. You can recover from almost anything, even self-induced panic. Once you see that today is the opportunity to build a better tomorrow, do not take tomorrow's joy away.

Asking Better Questions

You want to ask a question that elicits a conversation among professionals. Binary questions—those that can be answered by a yes or a no—are non-starters. They tend to kill conversations rather than open them up. Ask open-ended questions and you'll find you're having much better conversations.

Three-to-One Feedback

When asked for input and you see too much that's wrong with the book, pick your input wisely. Crushing people's souls isn't what anyone wants to do. A tried measure of delivering feed-back is give three positives for every opportuni-ty for improvement. Find those three things and only pick one that could be better. This assumes that the author asked for feedback, of course. Re-member that any unsolicited feedback is criticism.

Learning

Everything you've done before is the foundation for what you do today and the springboard for where you go tomorrow. You cannot change the past, but you can and must learn from it if you are to move forward. We learn more from our failures than our successes because we don't wish to re-peat mistakes. Successes are more difficult to build on because we don't always know why something succeeded.

Wealth Isn't Happiness

But you need money to survive in today's soci-ety. You can have a great time writing books, but you do have to treat your authoring as a business to get the most from it—and that includes rev-enue. Don't be fooled by the statement that mon-ey doesn't bring happiness. It absolutely creates the conditions where you can be happier by doing less of the painful stuff and more of the fun stuff.

A Rising Tide Lifts All Boats (Part Two)

Don't hold yourself back. Believe in yourself and commit to the hard work that needs to be done to get you where you want to go. There are no limits for those who want something badly enough. Join us and keep climbing the mountain of success. Your path is not ours and ours is not yours, but reaching back helps you take a step you may not have managed on your own. You still have to climb, but you're not on your own.

Be Yourself

All you, but a better version of you. As an author, you can be anything you want to be (that's within your control). You can even be rich and famous if you act like you're rich and famous and also write incredible stories that appeal to gob-loads of people. Envision it and then do the work that takes you there. Honestly, it's too hard to be someone else, so be the best version of yourself you can be and let that shine through to your readership.

The Decline of Material Consumption

The biggest lesson of 2020 is that people have grown to appreciate what we had taken for granted—the ability to be with others, enjoy a big conference with our peers, do readings, visit family. This goes to our business. We're the artisans who entertain, the insiders who educate. We have a greater role to play in a new world. Keep engaged the minds of those who are down. Experiences are what people miss most, and that is what a book provides.

Motivation—Doing What It Takes to Get Where You're Going

Small steps are still steps forward. Any step is a good step, except the one that takes you backward. Visualize where you want to be, even if you can't see the path to get there. Then look from that point to now. You'll see stepping stones. Lots of them. It's okay. Look at those who have gone before you. They've taken the steps. Your goal is achievable, but you have to take the steps. It may take longer than you want, but won't the end result be worth it?

How Long Do I Keep Going?

That's a hard question that demands more hard questions. Are you losing faith because you have written many books but aren't making any money? That can be depressing, but what have you done to improve your craft and your business from one book to the next? Professionals constantly train to get better at what they do. What feedback are you getting from one book to the next? Are you staying in the same genre to build readership? Are you writing books in a series where the first book doesn't sell? Are you panicking or are you analyzing? Temper your expectations based on your level of professional engagement.

Turn Your Experience into Wisdom

The only way to gain wisdom is if you learn from your experience. If you keep doing the same thing, you'll get the same result. If you take a critical look—not to criticize but to see what worked and what didn't—then you're well on your way to being older and wiser. Well, you're going to get older, no matter what. Wiser? That's up to you.

The Right Time May Not Be Right Now

You need your day job to pay bills and for healthcare. You're trying to write and the universe is conspiring against you. When is the right time to start your author career? Be honest with yourself – writing should relieve stress in your life, not add to it. When the time is right and the story is bursting from you like an alien fighting its way out of your stomach, then you'll know. In between, plot, gather story ideas, learn about newsletters, go to a conference or a writing retreat. Start building the foundation of a career for when the time is right.

What quotes and sayings are important to you? Jot them down. This book is about helping you to think about things that are important for your business.

_____

• _____

• _____

•

-

-

-

-

-

-

-

-

-

-

-

-

-

-

-

-

-

-

-

-

-

-

-

-

-

Postscript

If you liked this book, please give it a little love and leave a review. I'm not big on non-fiction. My wheelhouse is science fiction and thrillers! So, you don't need to join my newsletter as I'm not going to promote non-fiction there. But if you like sci-fi...

Please join my newsletter (https://craigmartell e.com), please, please sign up!), or you can follow me on Facebook. If you have any comments, shoot me a note at craig@craigmartelle.com. I am always happy to hear from people who've read my work. I try to answer every email I receive.

If you liked the story, please write a short review for me on Amazon. I greatly appreciate any kind words. Even one or two sentences go a long way.

The number of reviews an eBook receives greatly improves how well it does on Amazon.

Author exclusive Five-Minute Focus videos on YouTube (for free). These are focused author sessions to help you each and every day within the time constraints afforded busy professionals:

FMF Part 1 (Episodes 1-300) - https://www.youtube.com/playlist?list=PLnc BZIdgLIpl-BW_r19JjOfTmVi80mWoO

FMF Part 2 (Episodes 301-600) - https://www.youtube.com/playlist?list=PLnc BZIdgLIpnUaogGjlVDOdjHLyQDDoo8

FMF Part 3 (Episodes 601+) - https://www.youtube.com/playlist?list=PLnc BZIdgLIpmoaIWmh-qamnrA8AVdjWU0

Follow me in any of the places below or simply join my newsletter.

Amazon—https://www.amazon.com/author/c raigmartelle

BookBub—https://www.bookbub.com/autho rs/craig-martelle

Facebook—https://www.facebook.com/autho rcraigmartelle

In case you missed it before, my web page—https://craigmartelle.com

Author Notes

I am the blue-collar author. I have a law degree, but that doesn't matter, not when it comes to writing. What matters is the willingness to work hard at this thing called self-publishing. I've worked harder, not smarter, on a number of things. I've been fairly successful, but I have so much more to learn.

Part of what helps me learn is trying to help others. That's what this book is all about. I am sharing what I've done, and I've made many mistakes, some more costly than others. I want to help you avoid those mistakes while also telling you that you aren't alone.

Some of the other authors I reference are friends, and that is the strangest of things. When

I was fifty-one-years old, I was freezing my ass off on the North Slope of Alaska, inside the Arctic Circle, working as a business consultant in the oilfields. Now, I have friends who are household names in the publishing industry. I know people who are at the top of their genre lists, and sometimes, the book up there is the one I wrote. It's crazy how things can happen when you realize what you were meant to do.

But I wouldn't be me without all of the stuff in between. I don't think I could write compelling combat scenes without having been in war. I couldn't have written how that affects people without having witnessed it firsthand. It's all fun and games until you get issued grenades.

And the lawyer in me says that I should help people who are less inclined to enjoy reading statements from the IRS or your state's department of trade and business.

So, here I am, trying to share what I've learned. Although writing is a lonely profession, you don't have to be alone, just like I wasn't in writing this book.

Shout out to the proofreading crew! What a great bunch of people.

Jordan Barnes

Siobhan Purcell

Kel Gay

Angela Lucio King

Other Series by Craig Martelle

<u>**#—AVAILABLE IN AUDIO, TOO**</u>

(#) (co-written with Michael Anderle)—a post-apocalyptic paranormal adventure

Gateway to the Universe (#) (co-written with Justin Sloan & Michael Anderle)—this book transitions the characters from the Terry Henry Walton Chronicles to the Bad Company

The Bad Company (#) (co-written with Michael Anderle)—a military science fiction space opera

Judge, Jury, & Executioner (#)—a space opera adventure legal thriller

Shadow Vanguard—a Tom Dublin space adventure series

Superdreadnought (#)—an AI military space opera

Metal Legion (#)—a military space opera

The Free Trader (#)—a young adult science fiction action-adventure

Cygnus Space Opera (#)—a young adult space opera (set in the Free Trader universe)

Darklanding (#) (co-written with Scott Moon)—a space western

Mystically Engineered (co-written with Valerie Emerson)—mystics, dragons, & spaceships

Metamorphosis Alpha—stories from the world's first science fiction RPG

The Expanding Universe—science fiction anthologies

Zenophobia (#) (co-written with Brad Torgersen)—a space archaeological adventure

Battleship Leviathan (#)– a military sci-fi adventure published by Aethon Books

Starship Lost (#) – a hard science fiction space opera published by Aethon Books

Glory (#) (co-written with Ira Heinichen)—hard-hitting military sci-fi

Black Heart of the Dragon God (co-written with Jean Rabe)—a sword & sorcery novel

End Times Alaska (#)—a post-apocalyptic survivalist adventure published by Permuted Press

Nightwalker (a Frank Roderus series)—A post-apocalyptic Western adventure

End Days (#) (co-written with E.E. Isherwood)—a post-apocalyptic adventure

Successful Indie Author (#)—a nonfiction series to help self-published authors

Monster Case Files (co-written with Kathryn Hearst)—A Warner twins mystery adventure

Rick Banik (#)—Spy & terrorism action-adventure

Ian Bragg Thrillers (#)—a hitman with a conscience

Published exclusively by Craig Martelle, Inc

The Gygax Odyssey by Luke Gygax and J. Clifton Slater—a historical fiction retelling of the Gary Gygax family (co-creator of Dungeons & Dragons®)

The Dragon's Call by Angelique Anderson & Craig A. Price, Jr.—an epic fantasy quest

A Couples Travels—a nonfiction travel series

Love-Haight Case Files by Jean Rabe & Donald J. Bingle—the dead/undead have rights, too, a supernatural legal thriller

Loki Redeemedby Bruce Nesmith—the creator of Elder Scrolls V: Skyrim brings you Loki in the modern day, staying true to Norse Mythology (not a superhero version)

Mark of the Assassins by Landri Johnson—a coming-of-age fantasy.

For a complete list of Craig's books, stop by his website—https://craigmartelle.com

BVPRI - #0008 - 080125 - C0 - 203/127/6 - PB - 9781953062819 - Gloss Lamination